Willie Mays

A Little Golden Book® Biography

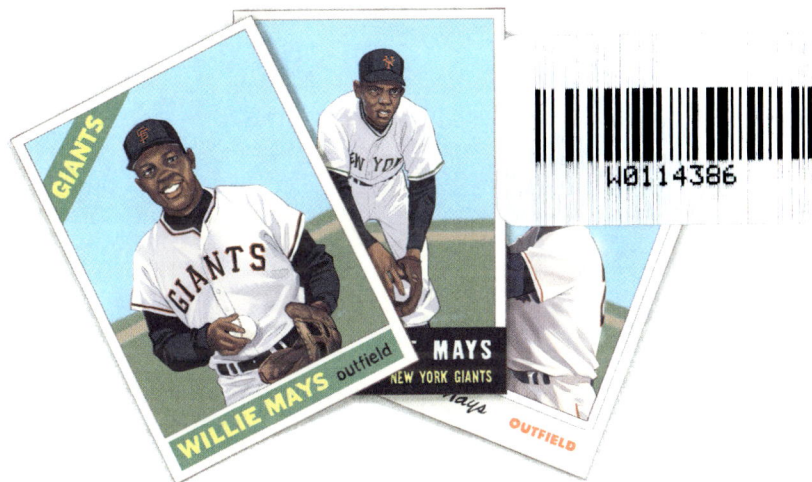

By Anne Wynter
Illustrated by Bea Jackson

A GOLDEN BOOK • NEW YORK

Text copyright © 2024 by Anne Wynter
Cover art and interior illustrations copyright © 2024 by Bea Jackson
All rights reserved. Published in the United States by Golden Books, an imprint of
Random House Children's Books, a division of Penguin Random House LLC, 1745 Broadway,
New York, NY 10019. Golden Books, A Golden Book, A Little Golden Book, the G colophon,
and the distinctive gold spine are registered trademarks of Penguin Random House LLC.
rhcbooks.com
Educators and librarians, for a variety of teaching tools, visit us at RHTeachersLibrarians.com
Library of Congress Control Number: 2024940853
ISBN 978-0-593-81329-4 (trade) — ISBN 978-0-593-81330-0 (ebook)
Printed in the United States of America
10 9 8 7 6 5 4 3 2 1

Willie Howard Mays Jr. was born on May 6, 1931, in Westfield, Alabama. Baseball was a part of his life from the very beginning. In fact, Willie learned to walk by chasing after a baseball! When he got older, his father showed him how to hit a rubber ball with a small stick. During games of catch, Willie's father explained every single baseball position.

Willie became so good that by the age of sixteen he was playing professional baseball for the Birmingham Black Barons, a team in the Negro leagues. Still a high school student, Willie promised his principal he would never miss a day of school because of baseball. He only traveled to away games during summer break.

The Negro league was a baseball league made up of Black players. Many of them—like Willie—were some of the best in the country. In Willie's first year with the Black Barons, they won the Negro American League pennant and made it to the Negro League World Series.

One day, a scout from the Major League team the
New York Giants came to watch Willie play. He
described Willie in a letter as the "greatest young
player I had ever seen in my life or my scouting career."

The Giants signed Willie to a contract soon after
his high school graduation.

Willie started off in the Giants minor league. He was the only Black player, and fans often shouted racist words at him. He dealt with segregation, which forced Black people and white people to use separate hotels and restaurants. That meant Willie spent a lot of time apart from his teammates. Sometimes he felt so lonely he thought about quitting.

It's a good thing he didn't. At age twenty, Willie officially became a center fielder for the New York Giants, wearing the number 24 on his uniform and playing home games at the Polo Grounds in New York City's Upper Manhattan.

Willie had finally made it to the Major Leagues!

According to the Giants team manager, Leo Durocher, a good baseball player needs to do five things: hit the ball, hit with power, run, field, and throw. Some professional players are good at two or three of those. Willie was amazing at all five.

Willie believed if you wanted to play your best, you had to have fun. Fans crowded into the stadium to see him fling the ball sidearm, secure a fly ball using his famous basket catch, and run around the bases so fast he'd lose his hat.

In Willie's first year, the Giants won the pennant and went to the World Series. Willie was named Rookie of the Year and picked up his famous nickname: the Say Hey Kid. It may have come from his early days on the team when Willie didn't know anyone's names and simply called out "Say hey!" to get their attention.

During his time with the New York Giants, Willie lived in Harlem. He loved playing stickball with the neighborhood kids, and he'd even buy them ice cream afterward.

Once, he was having so much fun with the kids, he forgot to show up for a game! A Giants team manager had to come find him and bring him to the ballpark.

In 1952, Willie was drafted into the army. He reported to Fort Eustis, Virginia, where he entertained the troops by playing baseball for a local team. He also taught soldiers how to throw, catch, and hit.

After serving two years in the army, Willie returned to the Giants and helped his team win the 1954 World Series. That season, Willie received the MVP award, the Male Athlete of the Year Award, and the Professional Athlete of the Year Award.

It was in the first game of the 1954 World Series that Willie made the famous play known as The Catch. Willie was in center field when the batter for the Cleveland Indians made a hit that soared way past Willie.

Willie ran at full speed, stopping just short of crashing into the outfield wall! He reached his arms out, let the ball drop into his glove, and—in a split second—launched it back to the infield. Many believe it was one of the greatest moments in sports history.

In 1957, Willie moved to California when the New York Giants became the San Francisco Giants. He had a tough time buying his first house because the neighbors didn't want to live near a Black family. Years later, when he moved to a home in a different part of the city, Willie finally received a warm welcome: a mailbox stuffed with letters from excited neighborhood kids.

After a difficult start, Willie got used to living and playing in San Francisco. During the Giants' 1965 season, he became the fifth player in baseball history to hit five hundred home runs. And in 1966, he hit his 512th home run, breaking the National League home run record!

In 1972, Willie was traded to the New York Mets. Even though leaving the Giants made him sad, New York fans were thrilled to welcome Willie back The next year, the Mets went on to win the pennant. Unfortunately, they lost to the Oakland A's in the World Series.

After twenty-two years in the major leagues, and with 660 home runs, Willie announced that he was done playing baseball.

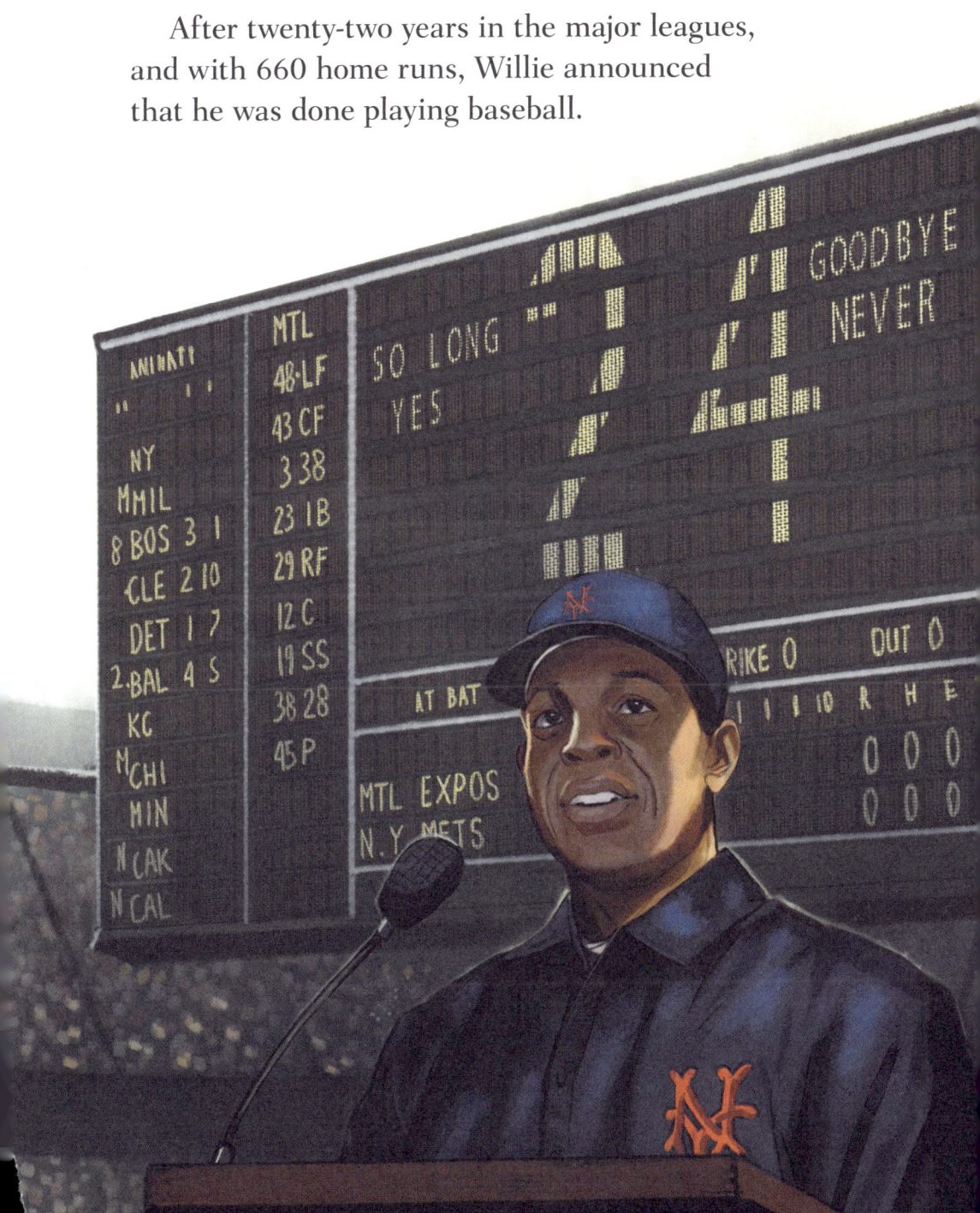

The honors and celebrations continued. Willie was inducted into the Baseball Hall of Fame in 1979. His uniform number was retired by both the Giants and the Mets—no other player on those teams can wear number 24. Fans who go to Giants home games are welcomed to the stadium by a nine-foot-tall statue of Willie. And he received the Presidential Medal of Freedom from President Obama in 2015.

Willie had a lifetime contract with the Giants and was always a beloved member of the team. They threw him a birthday celebration when he turned ninety years old.

Three years later, on June 18, 2024, Willie passed away. The sad news was announced during the sixth inning of a game between the Giants and the Cubs. Fans in the stadium responded by standing and applauding to honor the baseball legend.

Many believe Willie Mays was the best all-around baseball player ever. He will be remembered for his amazing athletic talent and his love of the game. Willie once said, "The game of baseball has been great to me." Fans of the Say Hey Kid see things the other way around: Willie Mays has been great to the game of baseball!